GRAND CONSTRUCTIONS

GRAND CONSTRUCTIONS

by Gian Paolo Ceserani
illustrated by Piero Ventura

G.P. Putnam's Sons, New York

Library of Congress Cataloging in Publication Data
Ceserani, Gian Paolo.
  Grand constructions.
  Translation of: Le grandi costruzioni.
  Summary: Presents in pictures and text the
great buildings and architectural highlights of
history, from Stonehenge to skyscrapers.
  1. Architecture—History. [1. Architecture—History] I. Ventura, Piero. II. Title.
NA200.C4413 1983 720'.9 82-12212
ISBN 0-399-20942-5
D. L. TO: 1380 -1983

Contents

Stonehenge

Stonehenge juts up dramatically on Salisbury Plain in southwest England. It is a complex of enormous stones that forms a complicated and puzzling design. Many of these monoliths (a word derived from the Greek, meaning "made from a single stone") are 23 feet (7 meters) in height and weigh as much as 30 tons. It is mind-boggling to think that these stones came from dozens of miles (tens of kilometers) away.

Although Stonehenge has always been a fascinating mystery, astronomers now believe this site was a sophisticated calendar used by people thousands of years ago. But many questions remain. When was Stonehenge built? How could these enormous stones have been transported to their present location? How were the people of ancient times able to erect this complex structure?

Surprisingly enough, the oldest living things on earth, the California redwood, have led to discoveries concerning these ancient stones. By counting the rings in a section of redwood tree trunk, scientists are able to determine the age of the tree. But after calculating the age of these ancient trees and comparing their conclusions with the carbon-14 method of determining age, which assumes that the amount of carbon present in the atmosphere has remained constant, scientists realized that the carbon-14 method was not totally accurate. Now they know that the carbon in the atmosphere has been constant for only the last 3,500 years.

This new knowledge stunned archeologists and historians. For the first time, they realized that the European megalithic monuments such as Stonehenge (megalithic from the Greek, meaning "large stone") were even older than they had thought.

Megalithic ruins are found along a belt that spreads east from Spain to Italy and Malta and north to France and England. Scientists know nothing about the great builders of the past who produced these structures and can only imagine the full scope and grandeur of their works. At Baalbek, Lebanon, there is an esplanade built from monoliths that weigh hundreds of tons each. At Sacsahuaman, Peru, there are town walls made from boulders the size of a room. Although no cement was used, the boulders in these dry walls are so perfectly fitted, it is impossible to insert even a knife between one boulder and another. On Ponape, an island in the Pacific, there is a strange construction made from blocks of basalt, a volcanic rock found neither on Ponape nor any island near it.

Scientists are staggered and awed by the amazing building skills and technical expertise demonstrated by the people of our remote past all over the world.

The First Houses

Although we know little about our most ancient ancestors such as the people who constructed Stonehenge, hundreds and hundreds of excavations all over the world have given us insight into how our ancestors lived during the long period when they were hunters and gatherers of herbs and roots, before the introduction of agriculture, a turning point in history that revolutionized human life.

For a long time it was believed that the people of the Paleolithic era (the second part of the Stone Age, the oldest period of human prehistory) lived a hard and uncomfortable life. The most recent discoveries make it clear that this was not necessarily so. The word "caveman" bears no relationship to the truth. Men seldom lived in caves, and when they did, it was only in certain areas and for reasons of climate. The cave, which was sometimes beautifully "air-conditioned," was more often the meeting place for the community or maybe the site of cult activities.

The inhabitants of this village lived on the shores of lakes and marshes in dwellings built on piles. This location provided them with readily accessible fish and water, as well as protection from animals. Their dwellings were comfortable, with wooden floors, often decorated with ornamental motifs, fiber mats and earthenware pottery. For protection, they even owned guard dogs!

Dwellings on dry land could be comfortable, too. They were built around a central hearth, with small basins dug out, which were filled with grass to make soft straw mattresses.

Man in the distant past overcame the harshest tests, always making use of his many skills to live in as much comfort and safety as possible.

Sumerian Ziggurats

For centuries people who traveled in the great desert region of Mesopotamia (the Iraq of today), would have noticed large hills of sand and crushed stone. Nobody ever guessed that these hills concealed the splendid monuments of the ancient civilization of Sumer.

However, ever since the nineteenth century, archeologists have been carrying out excavations to reconstruct this civilization, believed to be the oldest in the western world. They have discovered objects of daily use as well as thousands of inscribed tablets and hundreds of statues that depict kings and high priests with false beards and huge eyes. The archeologists have even reconstructed the most important Sumerian structure, the ziggurat, or temple.

The Sumerian civilization, which was a collection of city-states based on agriculture, flourished in the third and fourth centuries B.C. Because the most powerful force in its culture was religion, the greatest Sumerian buildings were the temples.

One of Man's Great Achievements

Man as a builder has had a long history. Nevertheless, we are still stunned when we see the enormous pyramid of Cheops in Egypt, which was built around 2,500 B.C. More than 100,000 men worked on it, transporting and erecting more than 2 million blocks of stone, each one weighing 2½ tons. When the pyramid was finished, it was 479 feet (146 meters) high, with each side of the base measuring 755 feet (230 meters).

Splendors in the Sand

When a pyramid was built, mounds of rubble were raised around the body of the structure, providing a base from which the men could work. When the pyramid was finished, the stone structure was covered with limestone, the peak of the pyramid was gold plated and the mounds of rubble were demolished. The limestone and gold plate, which sparkled in the sun, are long since gone, and today only the stone pyramid remains.

At Giza, near Cairo, there are three pyramids, Cheops, Chephren and Mycerine, named after the three pharaohs who ordered them built. The pharaoh was the supreme religious and civil authority in ancient Egypt, and the pyramid was designed to serve as his tomb.

Egyptians believed that existence continued after death if the body was preserved. Because of this, they developed highly sophisticated embalming techniques, and archeologists have discovered mummies which have been preserved perfectly for thousands of years. The pharaoh's body was carried in majestic procession into the tomb, where it was interred with precious jewels and great treasures. An ample supply of food was included for the dead one's journey to the other world.

Some people believe that the pyramids were more than tombs, particularly the pyramid of Cheops which some believe might have been built as a compendium, or summary, of the astronomical, geometrical and geographical knowledge of the Egyptian culture at that time. There have also been many theories about the similarities between the Egyptian pyramids and the pyramids that exist in pre-Columbian America.

The great works of Egypt, which include not only the pyramids, but also structures like those at Zoser, Karnak, Thebes and Abu Simbel, were made possible because of a strong, centralized state with efficient administration and unquestioned power.

The Greek Temple

The Greeks were among the greatest builders of ancient times, as well as among those with greatest influence. At various times throughout history, builders have returned to the elegance and simplicity of the classical Greek style. If you look around your own town or city, you will probably see examples of Greek-style architecture.

Among all the buildings of Greece, the temple was the most representative. The Greek temple was a miracle of symmetry and balance. The impressive columns in Doric, Ionian and Corinthian styles created striking contrasts between light and shadow. Certainly the Parthenon, the temple on the Acropolis in Athens, is the best known of all the Greek temples.

The Greek temple was more a religious site than a gathering place. Closed in by sacred walls, it was built in a secluded, isolated place, far from the city. In contrast to Roman basilicas or Christian churches, it was deliberately situated far from the road, usually on a hill or in some other dominant position where it would stand out in relief against the blue skies. Even today, when the original colors the temples were painted have vanished, the temples retain their splendor and impart a sense of majesty and religious intensity that stirs us deeply.

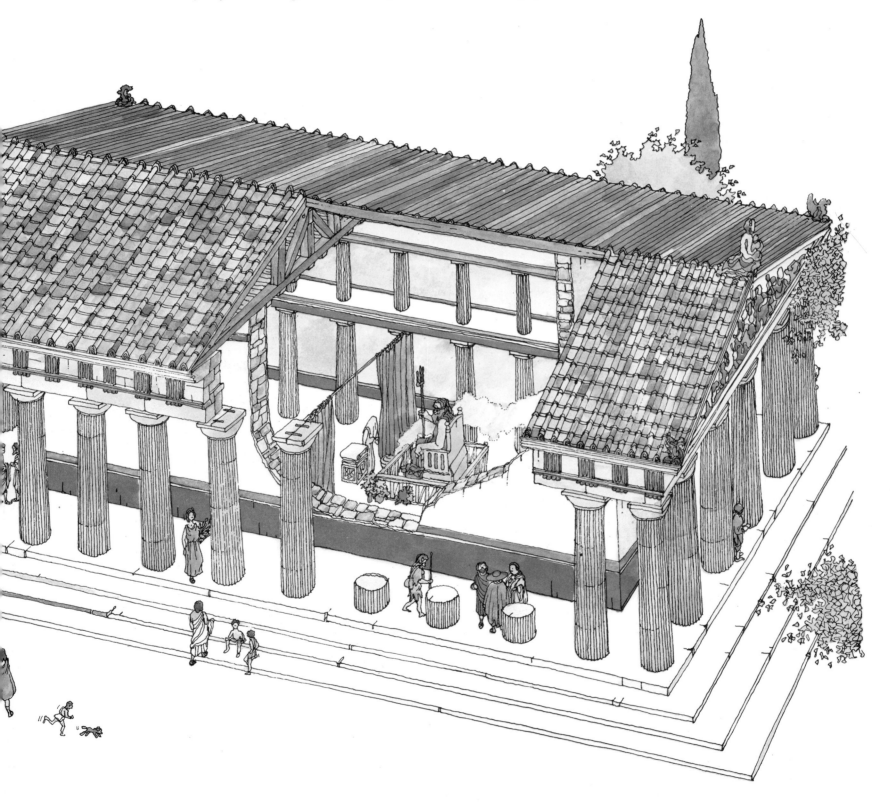

The Grandeur of Rome

Antiquity never saw a construction like the aqueduct at Rome. It was capable of carrying water from one end of the valley to the other at a considerable height. It was an impressive achievement, but a common one in the long period during which Roman civilization was dominant. Although we view the aqueduct with admiration, the Romans, a nation of builders, viewed it only as a functional structure. They didn't even bother to reshape stones that jutted out.

Rome was the capital of a huge empire that at its height in the third century A.D. stretched to Scotland on the north and to the Persian Gulf on the east, including most of North Africa and Arabia. The Roman Emperor was the ruler of most of the known world, and the empire needed an architecture that would express this power. The Roman theaters, basilicas, circuses, palaces, baths and villas were all designed to display success and power. It was during this period of the Roman Empire that "town planning" first came into existence, a deliberate designing of buildings and open spaces to foster a sense of grandeur.

The Romans became accomplished builders of roads, bridges, aqueducts and dams, and because they preferred solid and enduring materials, such as stone, brick and heavy blocks of concrete, their work survives to this day. The round arch was the fundamental principle behind all Roman architecture. It allowed the Romans to use small rocks to cover large surfaces. It is no wonder that when the emperors wanted to find a symbol of their glory, they built triumphal arches.

The Pantheon

The Roman architects also constructed great buildings utilizing the round arch. They installed a temporary wooden arch called a "centina" between two walls. Small-sized stones were placed on the centina in the shape of a wedge. When the last stone was in place and the arch was finished, the centina was dismantled. With this method, the Romans were able to build arches with a span of more than 79 feet (24 meters).

Vaults and cupolas were variations of the arch system. If the Roman builders constructed arches from either side of a building, they made the roof semicircular and it was called a circular vault. If they built in a circle, however, the arches met at a certain point in the center to form a cupola, or dome.

With a diameter of 142 feet (43.40 meters), the Pantheon today still has the largest cupola in the world. Pantheon means "all the gods," and the spherical form is a symbol of the cosmos. Inside, around the circular walls, statues of the divinities were placed in niches. The only source of light is the great "eye" of the cupola which is more than 30 feet (9 meters) in diameter and symbolizes the sun. The light, which shines dramatically down from the eye, serves as a spotlight. Luckily, the Pantheon, which was built in two phases, the first under Emperor Augustus, between 27 B.C. and A.D. 14, and the second under Emperor Hadrian, between A.D. 118 and 128, has been preserved perfectly so that we are able to admire its beautiful simplicity today.

The builders of every civilization have been influenced by the materials available to them. In Greece, marble was used. In France, limestone was available, in northern Europe many countries used wood. The Romans built mostly of limestone, and the Pantheon was no exception. The walls and roof were built of exceptionally fine limestone which was taken from volcanic earth known as "pozzolana."

The ingenuity of the Romans went beyond circular vaults. They also intersected two circular vaults above a squared span to produce the cross, or groin, vault. The cross vault had many advantages. Because the pressure was concentrated on the four corners of the covered area and not on the walls themselves, the builders were able to put large openings in the walls and also place windows beneath the arches. The cross-vault principle would be used for centuries to come, particularly in the great cathedrals and basilicas of Europe.

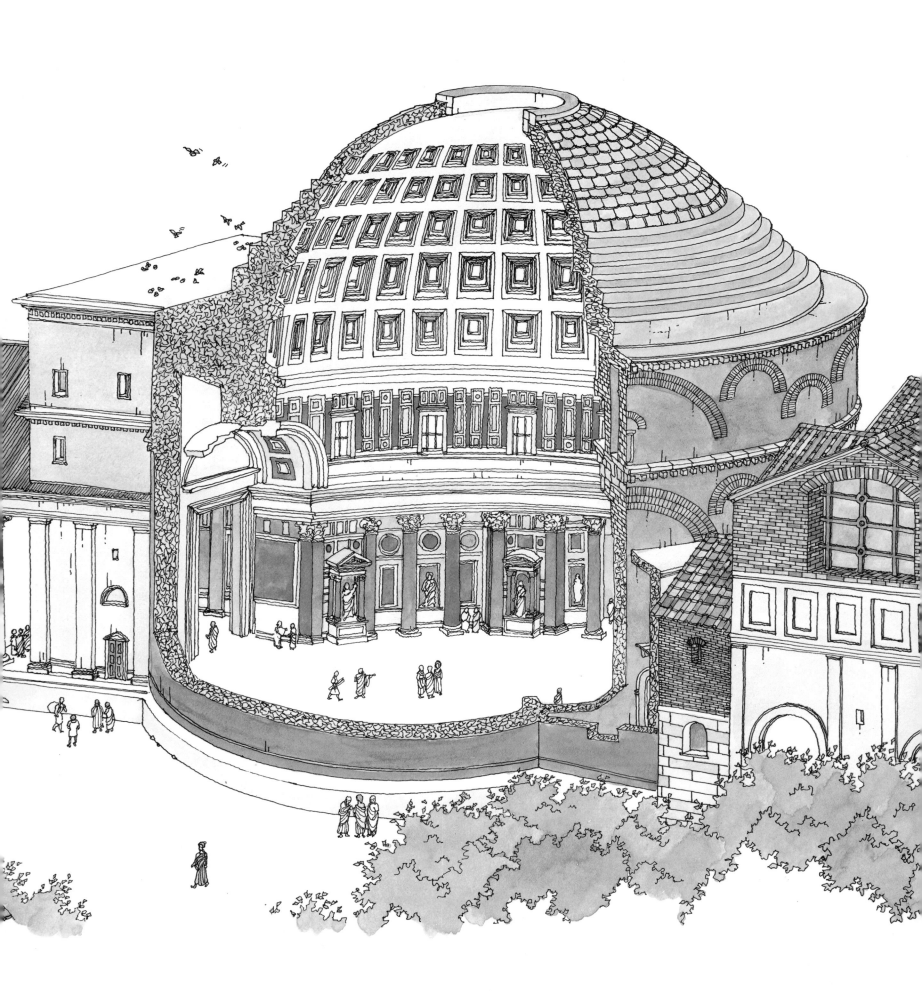

Rich Houses, Poor Houses

As a civilization, Rome was a city of great social differences and inequalities. Originally, the inhabitants of Rome were a small Latin tribe of farmers and shepherds. At its peak, Rome was *"caput mundi,"* that is, the greatest city in the world, with up to 2 million residents. It was rich in amphitheaters, baths and circuses. Three hundred fifty thousand spectators could fit into the Circus Maximus, and the Colosseum, the most famous amphitheater of all, could accommodate fifty thousand.

The maxim that governed the tumultuous life of Rome was *"panem et circenses,"* meaning bread and circus games. However, the free distribution of bread and the staging of spectacular events could not hide the great social differences between the people. The hills of Rome as well as the surrounding countryside and holiday villages were dotted with luxurious villas, but the capital itself was overcrowded, chaotic and lacking the most fundamental services.

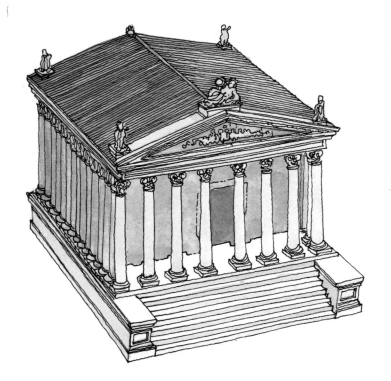

Tall houses called "insulae" were built for the Roman populace in parts of the city that were already overcrowded with shops and traffic. These uncomfortable houses, which were sometimes six stories high, lacked heating systems, hygienic services and running water. Unfortunately, the insulae were often built by dishonest builders who used inferior materials so that collapses and other disasters were common.

The home of the prosperous citizen was in direct contrast to the insulae. Its windows looked out onto an interior courtyard instead of onto the street. The Roman villa, a series of chambers and courtyards that circulated cool air, had bathrooms, dressing rooms, a swimming pool and a heating system that circulated hot air under

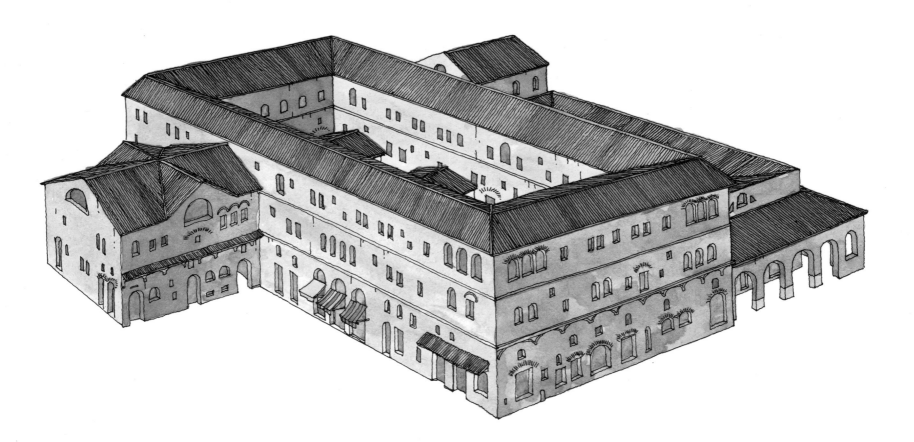

the stone floors and along the walls. Some of the more elaborate houses boasted valuable marble, precious mosaic floors and beautiful frescoes.

The disparity between classes grew to the point where the Roman Empire's strength and vitality was sapped. When the tribes of the north fell on Rome, they did not destroy a civilization, they destroyed an empire that had already been eaten away from within. In A.D. 476, when the last Roman emperor was deposed, the empire had long since ceased to be a living unit.

The Roads Part

Two events in the reign of the Roman Emperor Constantine changed the history of the world. In A.D. 313, Constantine recognized Christianity as the religion of the Roman Empire. In A.D. 330 Constantine, worried by the threat of northern tribes, moved the capital of the Roman Empire from Rome to the banks of the Bosporus. There he built a city named after him, Constantinople, which today is Istanbul. From that time on, history split in two. Even after the fall of Rome, Constantinople remained the Christian capital of the Byzantine Empire and continued as the capital until 1453 when it was conquered by the Turks.

A division in history also meant a division in culture. Byzantine architecture, whose influence was felt in the Byzantine Empire, parts of Italy and later in Russia, developed different characteristics from the architecture of western Europe. Primarily, there was the issue of churches. Christian religion needed a location for worship and it could not be built on the model of the temple. The temple was built strictly for the worship of a god, with sacrifices and processions taking place outside. In a church, space had to be found inside for the worshippers who gathered around the priest as he celebrated mass.

These new churches were designed along the lines of the basilica. The semicircular apse was built on the base from which the high altar was raised. The main chamber was called the nave; its extensions were called lateral naves. From the basilica, the Byzantine architects borrowed the principle of the cupola. The use of the cupola characterized the most important churches, Saint Sofia in Istanbul, Saint Mark's in Venice, and San Vitale in Ravenna, seen here. Eventually, the cupola was extended into a cluster of cupolas.

The decorative style of the Byzantine interiors was also distinctive. They were rich with marble and glittering with mosaics. Composed of millions of tiny pieces of marble or glass, these mosaics leave visitors breathless as they gaze up from the gloom of the church at the brilliant holy images.

A World Closes Off

Even in the fourth century A.D., a Roman citizen moved in an extensive and highly organized world. Merchants from everywhere came to his city or town to trade. He could travel for hundreds of miles and always find people who spoke his language and shared his culture.

The fall of the Roman Empire changed all that dramatically. The world was suddenly cut off. Communication became extremely difficult and the roads were soon unusable. Whereas before merchandise had come from all over the world, now a totally closed economy prevailed. Every town had to provide for itself, and its people were forced to become self-sufficient. For protection against the outside world, the typical medieval Italian village was built up on the peak of a hill surrounded by fortified walls. For many centuries to come, the medieval builder's primary task became that of insuring an adequate defense against outsiders.

Islam, a New Power

In the seventh century A.D., a new power from Arabia to the east, poured over a large part of the known world. The force of Islam, the religion founded by Mohammed, was powerful enough to build a huge empire which stretched from India to the Atlantic Ocean. Mohammed, the great prophetic figure who lived between the sixth and seventh centuries A.D., gave his people a sacred book, the Koran, and founded a religion that worshipped a single god. Mohammed created not only a religion, but a powerful and united nation as well.

Europeans watched in terror as the Arab armies moved up through Spain toward the rest of the continent. Although the Arabs' advance was halted, for a long time much of Spain remained in Muslim hands. Even today one can see in Spain splendid examples of Islamic art, such as the Alhambra.

The center of the Muslim religion is the mosque, a house of prayer. The first mosque, built in A.D. 622 in Medina, was Mohammed's house. Like other Arab houses, it was designed with a large courtyard surrounded by four walls. Enriched by the minbar (the pulpit for preaching), the minaret (a tower from which the summons to prayer was cried), porticos, courtyards and fountains, mosques, such as the royal mosque of Isfahan shown here, became ever more elaborate.

The Monastery

The medieval world, which no longer had a central stability, now turned to religion. Not only was religion a powerful spiritual force in the communities of Europe, but its monasteries also became models of organization and efficiency.

A community of self-governing and self-sufficient monks, who had voluntarily isolated themselves from the world, lived in a monastery. The monastery, which was often built in a picturesque setting, was a cultural site, a place of prayer and a model farm as well. Peasants, gardeners and craftsmen lived and worked among the monks in various buildings on the grounds. In addition to the cloisters, the church and the library, there was a kitchen, a bakery, a dining hall, various storehouses, a drying-house for the malt, stables, an ale-house, a herbalist's shop, an infirmary, a pharmacy, baths, grain-stores, mill-stores, stalls for the sheep, goats, cows and pigs, as well as dormitories for the monks and workers and guest rooms for visitors.

In the sixth century A.D., Benedict of Nursia founded the Benedictine Order of monks. Benedict gave the first community of monks a set of principles known as the "Rule" which organized monastic life from dawn to dusk down to the smallest detail. Their famous motto was "ora et labora," prayer and work. And that was how they lived, alternating prayer with a series of tasks, work and study. Our clock-regulated way of life has evolved from their efficient and structured existence. Civilization also owes the monks a debt of gratitude for preserving and copying the books and documents of the past. Without their efforts, much of our knowledge of earlier eras would have been lost.

The Romanesque Cathedral

For a long period of time, medieval culture was centered in the monasteries. At the turn of the millennium (A.D. 1000), the monastic orders began to build churches all over Europe. For instance, the Abbott Hugo of Semur approved plans for building more than a thousand churches. These churches, which were Romanesque in style, were imposing structures that dominated a landscape of small, low buildings.

"Romanesque" refers to the building principles that had been typical of the Roman civilization—the width of the basilica, the cross vault, and the wide, low, round Roman arch. But unlike the basilica, the Romanesque church had towers that soared proudly toward the sky. These towers were made possible by the development of the ribbed vault, which reinforced the cross vault. The builders created a "net" of arches that were joined together by small sized stones. Because they were able to fill the space between the arches with light material, they could lighten the supports, and this in turn enabled churches to reach new heights.

Since torches, oil lamps and candles provided the only illumination in medieval interiors, the risk of fire from these sources was great. Therefore the wood of Roman basilicas and Byzantine churches was supplanted in Romanesque churches by stone.

Stone buildings had a bare, harsh look, so to offset this, Romanesque churches gave the art of sculpture tremendous impetus. Almost every stone was sculptured with reliefs, flutings and pilasters, and beautiful sculptured capitals (the head of a column or pilaster), bas-reliefs and statues were common.

During the medieval period, pilgrims on religious journeys were a real force behind the building of Romanesque cathedrals and churches. Cathedrals became sanctuaries and stopping-places for the pilgrims, who often traveled in groups of hundreds for months at a time. Traveling alone was dangerous, so it was not unusual for a man to have journeyed with other pilgrims across Europe but never to have visited the village next to his own. The medieval age was a harsh and difficult period and the severe stone Romanesque churches made a fitting symbol for the times.

The Gothic Cathedral

Even though the thirteenth-century traveler had heard much about the magnificent Gothic cathedrals, when he first saw one towering above the landscape from a long distance away, he must have been awestruck. And well he might. These giants in stone, which were built on new architectural principles, seemed to be a product of sheer faith between the builder and his materials.

Because the Romanesque cathedral was built on the principle of the rounded arch and needed solid walls to support the stone vault, it could rise just so high and no higher. Now, with the new ogive, or Gothic arch, cathedrals could reach incredible heights. The ribbed vault allowed the ogive arch to support the strain of the weight vertically toward the base as well as laterally along the rampant arches and external buttresses. The cathedral at Beauvais is an example of the height attained—it soared 158 feet (48 meters) into the sky.

The ogive arch not only permitted churches to climb, but it also allowed the use of much lighter walls. For the first time huge windows became possible, and the Gothic cathedrals developed into enormous, luminous glass houses with their breathtakingly beautiful stained glass windows.

The Gothic cathedral, however, was not simply a result of new technical know-how; it was also a manifestation of the theology of the times. The cathedral symbolized the need to raise God up, while at the same time diminishing man. Certainly when a man of medieval times entered a cathedral, he felt diminished indeed. The vault was so high it seemed to stretch upward forever. The stained glass glittered like precious stones. The pillars sparkled like gold, and the statues of the saints stared sternly down. Even today a visitor often feels overwhelmed when he enters one of these awesome cathedrals.

The Gothic style originated in northern France, but it soon conquered most of Europe. A city's greatest pride was its cathedral, and there was often fierce competition as to which city possessed the most impressive structure. In France, Chartres, with its two towers, is the most famous cathedral of all. Notre Dame, Amiens, Bourges, Lyons and Rouen cathedrals bring visitors to France from all over the world, as do the famous cathedrals of England, Germany, Belgium and Spain. The Gothic cathedral to this day remains a high point in the history of architecture.

The Master Builders

The cathedral was a living monument raised for the glory of God, so the man in the street often worked on it without pay for reasons of faith. But it took more than workers to build a cathedral. First of all, there had to be money. To a great extent, the clergy provided the capital, with the city's increasingly powerful middle classes contributing to a lesser extent.

The word cathedral is derived from the Latin *cathedra*, which means the throne of the bishop, and certainly the bishop played the most significant role. He was aided by a group of other churchmen who together made up a chapter. The master builder, the most important person in the construction of a cathedral, was appointed by this chapter.

The master builder was a specialist who was highly paid and much sought after. Today he would be called an architect, although in reality, he was much more. He was the driving force behind the great work, who not only planned the building, but also invented the machines for loading and unloading the stone and timber, supplied the sculptors with the outline of the sculptures, selected the workmen and directed the work yards. And his influence was wide. During the intensely religious thirteenth and fourteenth centuries, travel in Europe was relatively easy, much as it is today. Because these master builders traveled all over Europe, their ideas and techniques spread, making Gothic architecture an international style. Nevertheless,

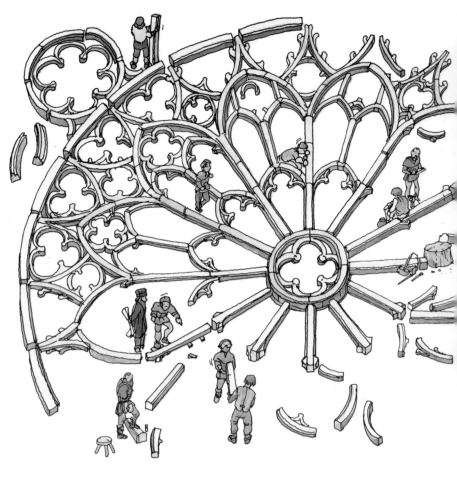

highly esteemed as the master builders were, at the time they were not considered true artists and consequently, almost none of their names have come down to us.

The master builder was also responsible for selecting the master craftsmen who would work with him, sculptors, glass-workers, carpenters, tinsmiths, forgers, stonebreakers and masons. Special recognition was given to the glass-makers who prepared the stained glass for the enormous windows and the all-important large rose-window in the façade. Because the whole cathedral was sculptured inside and out, the sculptors were highly regarded, too.

Work houses were constructed where the men lived, rested, ate and worked during bad weather. One of the greatest problems was transporting the huge blocks of stone and the long posts for the scaffolding, which often had to come by sea. All in all, building a cathedral was an incredibly slow and difficult task that sometimes took more than a century to complete.

The Castle

More than any other building, the castle, in its
isolation, has come to represent the long
centuries of the medieval period. Built on the
crest of a hill, the castle looked straight down
into the valley below. Squat buildings clustered
on its wide walls. The bastions and towers, as
well as its thick walls, protected the castle within.
Often a village of humble houses tucked itself in
around the outside castle walls in order to take
advantage of the protection the stone colossus
afforded.

The first castles, which were built strictly for
defense, were protected by ditches, drawbridges,
slopes, portcullises (iron gratings over gateways
that were lowered to prevent passage), and
crenellations, which were embrasures (openings
in the wall to allow firing cannon) and merlons
(solid wall intervals alternating between
embrasures). Seizing a castle was almost
impossible. Because a castle was constructed to
resist every kind of attack, a few hundred men
inside could drive back the enemy. The only way
to take a castle was by laying siege to it for
months, or even years. Hunger, and, more often,
disease, would finally force the inhabitants to
surrender.

Gradually, however, times changed. The
invention of gunpowder made a difference in the
way wars were fought. Cities grew up again and
trading resumed. The character of the castle
changed too. It became a richer, more impressive
place, a luxurious residence, sometimes even a
palace. From that time on, the role of defense
was taken over by forts.

The City of Merchants

During the long medieval period, Europe was a continent of sparsely populated villages. Most of the inhabitants of these villages were serfs who were tied to the soil and, under the domination of feudal lords, had few rights.

Over a period of centuries, this village-oriented society began to change. As Gothic cathedrals became the pride of cities, the people who had contributed to their development became more important, and a middle class developed. As time passed, more and more serfs began to live and work in the cities.

The medieval city was small, with such narrow roads only foot travel was possible. But it soon became a center for artisans, or craftsmen—cloth-makers, dyers, carpenters, glass-makers, blacksmiths, candle-makers, masons, enamellists, engravers, artists and sculptors.

The artisans' houses were tied closely to their work. Their workshops or offices were on the ground floor with their living quarters above. Now the emerging city began to develop into a center of exchange. At first

commerce took place in the market where products from the surrounding
countryside were bought, sold or traded. Very quickly, however,
particularly in such cities as Venice, Genoa, Pisa, Milan, Bruges,
Ghent, Ostend and London, goods were being bought and sold from all
over the known world, including the Orient.

By today's standards, these medieval cities were small, usually with no
more than 50,000 inhabitants. But they were rich. Their buildings
included not only churches, but palaces, company offices, colleges and
universities as well. And the merchant middle class within the cities
became more and more powerful.

The artists and craftsmen in the cities began to assume power, too.
They organized themselves into guilds. Each craft had its own guild that
not only protected its members and guaranteed them a market for their
products, but also prevented craftsmen outside the city from working
within the city. On the one hand, the cities were open to trade; on the
other hand, they were extremely protective of their own rights.

Brunelleschi's Cupola

The growing power of the merchants was vital to the development of that period in history known as the Renaissance. If the Gothic movement was French, the Renaissance movement was Italian. It was in Italy that this new class of mercantile aristocracy evolved. With unprecedented wealth and power, these "merchant princes" became the protectors and sponsors of artists. Consequently, they were pivotal in the rebirth, or new way of seeing the world, that was called the Renaissance.

The most powerful of these Italian princes were the Visconti and the Sforza in Milan, the Gonzaga at Mantua, the Montefeltro at Urbino and the Medici in Florence. The Medici above all are famous for the recognition and encouragement they gave to artists and their work. During a few short decades, the fascinating and influential Medici family advanced some of the world's greatest artists: Leonardo da Vinci, Botticelli, Donatello, Michelangelo, and architects like Alberti and Brunelleschi.

In 1420 the city of Florence announced a competition for the building of a great cupola over the already existing Duomo. The architect Filippo Brunelleschi whose style went back to the classical forms (columns, pediments, and cornices) won the contest. Brunelleschi was the only contestant who had indicated how the centering should be supported. He proposed raising it on a wooden platform, held securely to the cylinder by iron chains. Brunelleschi bound the cupola on the inside, inserting a series of wooden tie-beams strengthened with iron bands for support.

Although this procedure may sound strange today, it was the only possible solution at the time, and until the use of concrete five centuries later, no one was able to devise a better way. For a long time, Brunelleschi's cupola, which dominated the city of Florence, remained a model for Renaissance and Baroque churches. This was not only because of Brunelleschi's building technique but also because his cupola, powerful, yet high and slender, was considered the most elegant in the world.

The Architect Signs His Work

History knows little about the cathedral builders of medieval times, either as artists or people. But with the Renaissance, a new attitude emerged. The architect was now appreciated as an artist the same way a painter was. And the proof was that he began to sign his works. For the first time, the names of architects who designed certain buildings, as well as something about them as people, became known to history. Certainly many of their names will always be famous: Brunelleschi, Alberti, Bramante and Michelangelo. During the medieval period, a cathedral was named after the city where it was located, Chartres Cathedral, for example. Now structures such as Brunelleschi's cupola were named after the architect.

Until the Renaissance, the architect began his career in some other field, perhaps as a jeweler, a painter, a sculptor or a silversmith. Brunelleschi, for instance, began as a goldsmith. From the Renaissance on, however, architecture became a respected and honored profession. Instead of starting out in another profession, the architect now gained experience as a manual laborer, rising from the ranks until he eventually became a master architect. One of the greatest architects of the period was Leon Battista Alberti, who not only designed important works such as the Rucellai Palace in Florence, but was also a theorist.

A characteristic sign of the Renaissance was that for the first time the best known Italian architects were designing secular palaces and civic buildings. Traditionally, the churches had commissioned a builder's most notable works. Now the merchant princes, who wanted to create a culture of their own, were also commissioning important buildings, thereby contributing to the development of architecture as a profession. At the same time Brunelleschi was designing the cupola of the Duomo, he was also directing construction of the Hospital of the Innocents in Florence.

The Olympic Theater near Mantua, which was finished in 1589, is shown here. It was the work of Vincenzo Scamozzi. The Gonzaga family was the sponsor for this secular masterpiece. Its elegant and colonnaded interior represented two important principles of the times—the pride of the princely courts and the renaissance, or rebirth, of the motifs of the classical style.

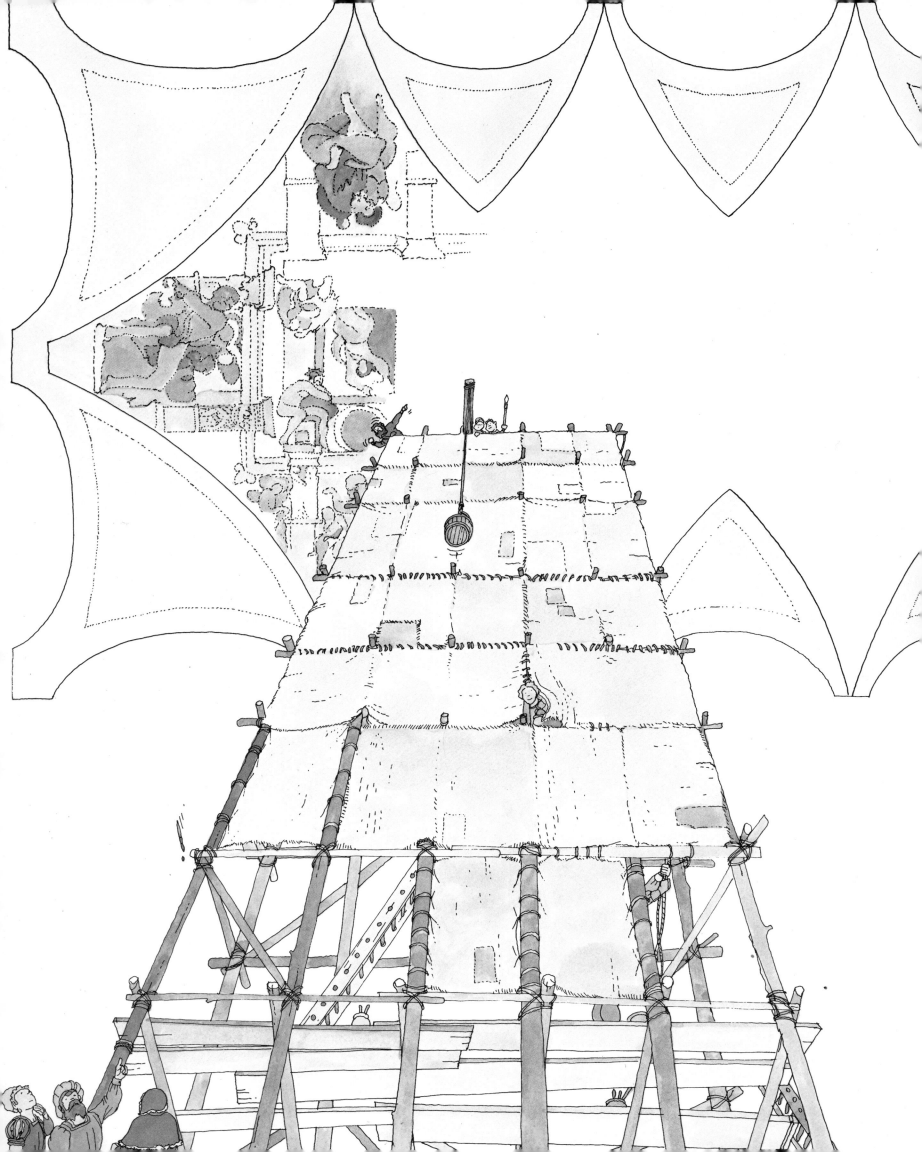

The Most Famous Ceiling in the World

When Michelangelo was offered the job of painting the vault of the Sistine Chapel in Rome, he was reluctant to accept. He considered himself to be a sculptor and an architect, not a painter. However, once he started, he closed himself up in the chapel and for four years worked alone, usually lying flat on his back on high scaffolding. His immortal masterpiece was a legendary achievement that astounds us to this day.

The Villas of Palladio

Andrea Palladio, a great architect who espoused the ideals of Greek and Roman classicism, lived for almost the whole sixteenth century. (He was born in 1508 and died in 1580.) Palladio was famous during his lifetime for the sophisticated, serene and balanced style of his churches, palaces and especially for his villas. These villas, such as Villa Barbaro at Maser, which you see here, were located in the Venetian countryside.

The cities were becoming noisy and crowded, and wealthy merchants craved the peace and quiet of the country. Because Palladio believed that everything had to contribute to the ideals of both classicism and serenity, he stressed the important relationship between the house and the gardens. Much had changed in just two centuries. Luxurious private villas were now designed for a tranquil and pleasant country life. Architecture had come a long way from the austerity of the medieval castle.

Palladio's style pleased not only his wealthy contemporaries, but people of a later period as well. In the eighteenth century, there was a return to classical principles, particularly in the English speaking countries. Tourists traveling in Italy were so impressed by Palladio's buildings that when they returned to England and America, they designed many churches and public buildings in the "Palladian" style.

The Pyramids of the New World

Christopher Columbus sailed the Atlantic Ocean in search of a new route to India. On the night of October 11, 1492, his expedition sighted land. But it was neither Japan nor China, as Columbus had hoped; it was a small island in the Bahama group. Instead of a new trade route, Columbus had discovered a continent.

Although the natives Columbus met were poor and primitive, a later expedition led by the Spaniard Hernando Cortes encountered the rich and highly sophisticated civilization of the Aztecs. Cortes, who left Cuba in 1519 to explore Mexico, was astonished to find that the Aztecs were a complex race of warriors, builders, traders and farmers. Although Cortes manned only a small expedition, 553 soldiers, ten cannons, and sixteen horses all traveling on eleven ships, he allied himself with tribes hostile to the Aztecs and defeated the Aztecs in a number of decisive battles. He

took King Montezuma captive and conquered the kingdom's capital.

Several factors contributed to the conquest of so many Aztec warriors by so few Spaniards. It was not only that the Aztecs were terrified of the cannons and horses, which they had never seen before, but they were confounded by the Spaniards' totally alien culture.

The Spaniards were amazed to find that the immense and splendid Aztec capital, Tenochtitlán (present day Mexico City), was built on canals like Venice with a large and thriving marketplace. They were also astounded by the huge sacred complexes of Monte Albán and by Teotihuacán, a sacred city with many temples, buildings and great streets. Two enormous pyramids were named after the sun and the moon. The Pyramid of the Sun (shown here) was 213 feet (65 meters) high and 722 feet (220 meters) wide at the base.

Mystery City

Like Cortes before him, the Spaniard Francisco Pizarro also conquered an empire in the New World, the Kingdom of the Incas. In September 1532, Pizarro, with less than 200 men, crossed Peru, a country of enormous geographical variety. Under Pizarro, the small band traveled from the sea to tropical jungle to the eternally snow-capped peaks of the Andes mountains.

This was the land of the Incas, a people who had already reached a high level of civilization. For hundreds of miles, great roads criss-crossed their country, scaling mountains and fording abysses with bridges that were built with skill and daring. Thousands of Inca couriers served as links connecting one section of Peru with another. By using these roads, couriers could deliver fresh fish from the sea to an inland city with an elevation of 13,000 feet in just one day.

Following Cortes's example, Pizarro and his band of men conquered the country. He ambushed and captured the Inca king Atahualpa, then demanded an enormous ransom in gold and silver. Always searching for the Incas' treasure, the Spaniards fought their way through all of Peru. Even when the Inca Empire had collapsed in defeat, the Spaniards ransacked and pillaged in their desperate quest for gold.

Only Machu Picchu eluded them. Machu Picchu was a fortress-city perched like the nest of an eagle on a peak in the Andes at an elevation of 13,000 feet. The city was so inaccessible, it wasn't located until 1911, when an American, Hiram Bingham, discovered it. Cut out of rock and surrounded by incredible precipices, Machu Picchu had been uninhabited for centuries. It was one of the most dramatic finds in the history of archeology.

The Maya

Two expeditions of daring and unscrupulous men had succeeded in destroying the great empires of the Aztecs and the Incas. But when Europeans arrived in the thick jungle of the Yucatán on the Mexican peninsula, the great civilization that had once thrived there was fading.

The Maya, who were the only people known to have built a complex civilization in a tropical jungle, left many questions behind. Although Europeans came upon the evidence of their civilization in the sixteenth century, some time thereafter the Maya literally disappeared from human memory. By the middle of the nineteenth century, the name of these people was not even known. And then, around 1840, two New Yorkers, Stephens and Catherwood, undertook to rediscover the Maya.

Stephens and Catherwood unearthed thick vegetation to reveal powerful stone buildings of an extraordinary level of architecture. When the two men reached Palenque, one of the main Mayan centers, they found great temples hidden by tangles of vines and creepers, with trees growing from the temple steps. Now the interest of the general public was aroused. Gradually, a series of cities and buildings was brought forth: Palenque, Copan, Tikal, Uxmal, Chichen Itza.

The pyramidic temple, crowned by a sanctuary, was typical of the Mayan culture. A flight of steps so steep as to give the climber vertigo led the way up. For a long time, no one knew how the Maya developed such a great and advanced civilization without the use of the wheel or any other visible means of transportation. It is only recently we have learned that they built an elaborate network of canals through the forests to serve their transportation needs.

The Maya, as well as being gifted architects, also practiced advanced astronomy. Even more impressive was their mathematics, which included the number zero long before European mathematics did. They grew crops of maize and attributed so much importance to the calendar, they were referred to as having an "obsession with time." A mystery, however, still remains. We have never learned all the reasons this great civilization died.

St. Peter's

The basilica of St. Peter's in Rome is perhaps the best known monument in the world. In 1506 Pope Julius II appointed the great architect Bramante to reconstruct the old basilica. It would be one hundred years before the work was finished, and during that time, a roster of famous architects and artists worked on it including Bramante, Raphael, Sangallo, Peruzzi, and Michelangelo. The dome was the work of Michelangelo, although it was not finished until after his death. It is considered one of St. Peter's most beautiful features. Supported by ten girders, it is 246 feet (75 meters) high with a diameter of 138 feet (42 meters).

Many critics believe that the basilica itself lacks true architectural unity. Too many men, no matter how talented, worked on it, and for this reason, its disparate elements do not fuse into a unified whole. Other critics, however, point out that its unique grandeur and rich decoration make it appropriate for Christianity's principal church.

Much of the fascination with St. Peter's is due to its famous colonnade, St. Peter's Square, shown here. At the time of its construction by the architect Bernini in the mid-1600s, a new architectural style had developed, the Baroque style. Bernini, who was one of the great Baroque architects, had originally thought he would completely close off St. Peter's Square, but subsequently decided to frame the square with a great curved colonnade. In doing so, he achieved an extraordinary effect. The columns projected a deceptive perspective which completely immersed the spectator in the setting. The extravagant and grandiose Baroque style had come a long way from the classical severity of the Renaissance.

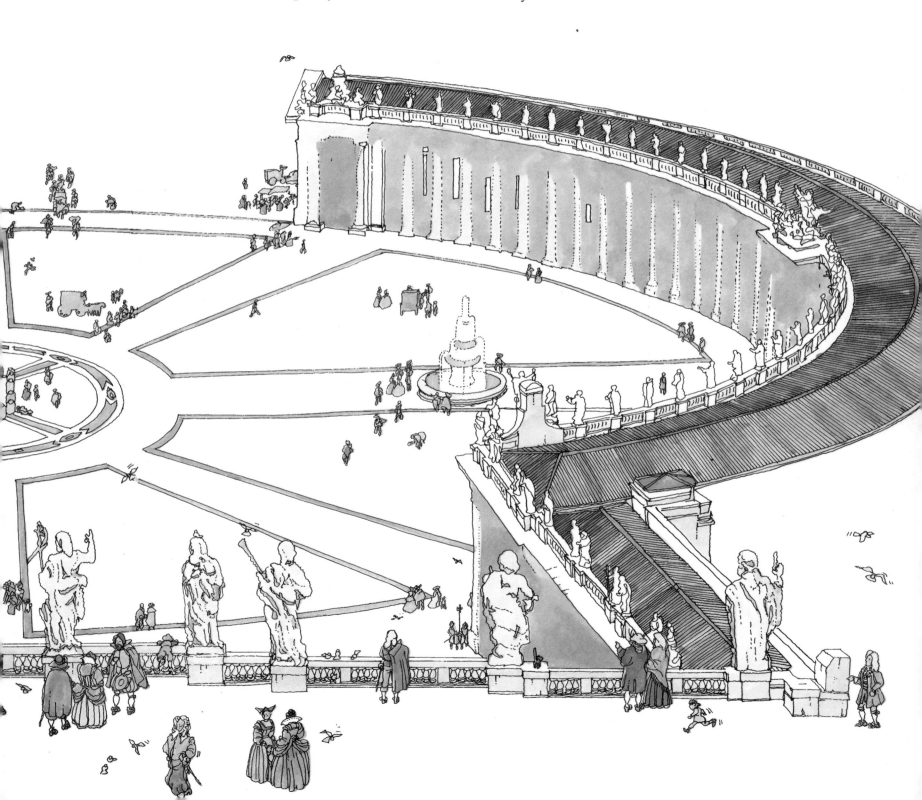

The Baroque

Many names that describe certain architectural styles were originally intended to be derisive. For instance, "Gothic," which referred to the barbaric Goths who had invaded the Roman Empire, was a derogatory term used by contemporary Italian critics who disliked the new Renaissance architecture.

The Spanish word "Baroco" was originally used to describe irregularly cut precious stones, but came to mean "absurd" and "grotesque." Consequently, the term "Baroque" was originated by those critics who preferred the traditional classical style.

The first Baroque building was the church of Santa Susanna in Rome which was designed by Carlo Maderno in 1600 at a time of a new surge in human creativity. In this building, colonnades, pillars, pediments and sculptures all rise toward one vertex. Its style was diametrically opposed to the Renaissance ideal of a round and symmetrical church.

This completely new way of interpreting architecture spread from Rome throughout Europe, although the three greatest architects of the Baroque period, Bernini, Borromini and Pietro da Cortona, worked mainly in Rome.

The Baroque style soon became a fantastic, dream-like art form. It used every architectural element, including fountains and gardens, to obtain spectacular effects. It is this quality which makes it great and also, claim its critics, what limits it.

The Escorial

The Spanish Baroque was famous for its richness and creativity, and the Spanish, in their conquest of the New World, took this architectural style with them. The Baroque triumphed in Mexico, and many impressive Baroque churches were built there.

Because the Baroque style was so popular in Spain, it seems strange that just before the Baroque period, such an austere complex as the Escorial was built near Madrid. Architecture, perhaps more than any

other art form, reflects the character of a monarch, and certainly the Escorial reveals a good deal about King Philip II under whose direction it was built. He was a somber and deeply religious man who reigned from 1556 to the end of the sixteenth century. The enormous Escorial, which rises up on a solitary hill, combines the characteristics of a palace and a monastery. It got its name from a little hamlet in the vicinity that furnished shelter to the workmen building it, and to the monks who eventually lived in its monastery.

Versailles

Just as the Escorial reveals the character of King Philip II, so Versailles, the palace of the French kings, reveals the character of King Louis XIV. Such grandeur had not been seen since the days of the Roman Empire. The growth of Rome, however, had been a gradual process, whereas the magnificence of seventeenth-century Versailles was the result of one monarch's tremendous centralized power.

Louis XIV, who said of himself, "I am the state," preferred to build his palace at Versailles rather than in Paris. Versailles was begun shortly after the middle of the seventeenth century and finished about a hundred years later. The façade, which was based on massive pillars, was more than 1,300 feet (400 meters) long. The interior of this spectacular complex included hundreds of apartments for the nobility, plus halls, chambers and the famous Gallery of Mirrors.

Perhaps even more than the architecture, the design of the Versailles gardens was important. The purpose of the gardens was to provide a relaxing atmosphere for the hundreds of nobles who spent all their days at leisure. There were artificial caves, temples, open air theaters, small lakes and water gardens. Of particular interest in terms of urban development and city planning are the series of long straight paths that meet forming a circle, and the network of roads that radiate out into the countryside. Versailles's huge gardens became the prototype after which the cities of the eighteenth century would be designed. Until this time, people had lived in cities with small, intricate street systems and tiny squares. From now on, cities would be planned with long avenues, large squares and streets built in radial patterns.

A City and Its Cathedral

In 1666 a devastating fire swept London for four days. Most of the houses were wood, and 13,200 dwellings and 89 churches were destroyed. The hard working London merchants set up their tents among the smoking ruins and soon were in business again. Living in London at the time was a 35-year-old architect, Christopher Wren, who was destined to become one of the most important names in the history of architecture. Wren, like an artist during the Renaissance period, was distinguished in several fields: architecture, astronomy and mathematics.

   The task of rebuilding London was assigned to Wren, and within two weeks, he had drawn up plans for a new city. They were totally original, with roads spreading out radially in ways that took the height of the buildings into account. His rational way of approaching the problem was a far cry from the maze of streets and alleys that were typical of the period.

Although his design for London ran into many obstacles and was never completely realized, Wren nevertheless created a marvelous city with church spires rising imaginatively above the small houses and everything dominated by the impressive mass of St. Paul's Cathedral.

Between 1670 and 1686, Wren built fifty-one churches, all marked with his distinctive style. Christopher Wren's greatest work was St. Paul's Cathedral. The old St. Paul's, which had been destroyed by fire, had been the longest church in the world. For the new cathedral, Wren prepared a model 20 feet (6 meters) long, which was both innovative and daring. Although the clergy wanted something more traditional, Wren was able to stamp his personal imprint on the new St. Paul's with its huge dome on eight pillars crowned by a high lantern. Wren, who had known Bernini, created a great Baroque structure which was considered to be the most notable building of its time.

More About the Baroque

The Baroque style, which mixed painting, sculpture, music and architecture in an explosion of fantasy, seldom went beyond the boundaries of Italy, Spain, Czechoslovakia, Austria and Bavaria. Because its ornate gaudiness was in direct contrast to the austerity of northern Europe's Protestantism, the Baroque style was never popular in the north. The more Baroque a style became, the more elaborate its design—perforated vaults, brighter and brighter colors, decorations of fruit, vegetation and shells. Every so often there was such bad taste exhibited, particularly in some of the homes of the lesser German nobility, that the Baroque merged with the Rococo style.

Despite occasional bad taste, there were great architects outside of Italy, like the Asam brothers and Johann Balthasar Neumann, all of whom visited Rome and were deeply impressed. Splendid buildings were designed in Austria, Bohemia and Bavaria. The episcopal palace in Würzburg, Bavaria, which was designed by Neumann around 1720 and built over a period of sixty years, is pictured here. It boasted fantastic stairs and an incredibly rich imperial hall decorated with the frescoes of Tiepolo.

A Capital for America

It was predictable that tastes would change. The people of the eighteenth century soon grew tired of the excesses of the Baroque, and there was a swing back to an old classical favorite, Palladio. In particular, eighteenth-century England returned to the Palladian style, and it was natural that America would follow England's lead. Even after the United States won its independence from England, America's interest in the Palladian style continued.

When Americans came to build their capital in Washington, D.C., many of the new buildings such as the White House and the Capitol Building were built along the simple and classical lines of ancient Greece. Although the Capitol was planned at the end of the eighteenth century, it was not completed as we see it today until fifty years later.

The Industrial Revolution

Of all the revolutions in the history of mankind, the Industrial Revolution was perhaps the most important in terms of our lives today. At the end of the eighteenth century, the first factories for the mechanical production of cloth were opened in Lancashire, in northwest England.

At first the primitive factories used water as their source of energy. Just a few decades later, however, factories utilized steam power for their new machinery, and England was convulsed by the unstoppable rise of industry. The United States, France, Germany, and other countries soon launched their own industrial revolutions.

A whole new era was born. Terrible slums multiplied, where thousands of people lived huddled together in inadequate buildings amidst the constant smoke from factory chimneys. Deplorable sanitary conditions compounded their misery.

But gradually, living and working conditions improved. Industry has come a long way from its original, inhumane beginnings. It is only today that we can appreciate that we owe many of the advances in our lives to the driving force of industry. Not only has advancing technology changed our civilization, but it brought about construction of buildings that would once have been considered impossible. For the first time, railways, buildings and bridges were made of iron and steel.

Building in Iron

At the time of the Industrial Revolution, architects did not immediately understand the possibilities of building with iron. Railways, viaducts and docks were essential for commerce but were not considered architecture. England, which was at the forefront of the Industrial Revolution, was at this time reviving Gothic architecture in the neo-Gothic style.

Because industry needed new functional designs, a new kind of builder was emerging, one who was an expert with materials and who could build in iron. This person was the engineer. Until now, the architect and the engineer had been one and the same.

At first people had trouble accepting iron as a building material, and if a structure was built in iron, it was often disguised. For example, an iron railroad station might be covered with a brick façade. It was only gradually that people realized that iron and architecture weren't incompatible.

The Brooklyn Bridge, which was the longest suspension bridge in the world and the first to use steel extensively, was completed in 1883. In 1889 the Paris Exhibition heralded the triumph of this new building principle in two structures made of iron and steel, the Eiffel Tower and the Galerie des Machines (shown here), a huge hall completely covered in glass.

The City "On Stage"

Cities in the nineteenth century were anxious to display the splendor of their monarchies. Each great city was truly a city "on stage." While its outskirts were rapidly changing and chimney stacks were beginning to fill the skies with smoke, the city center became the state's visible symbol of power.

These cities, built in the classical style, reminded one of the splendor of Imperial Rome. The French coined an appropriate word to describe this grandeur: *gloire*, meaning glory. In Paris, it was this feeling of *gloire* which gave birth to the Étoile with its imposing Arc de Triomphe and to such majestic buildings as the Opera, which we see here.

The Age of Reinforced Concrete

Toward the end of the nineteenth century, there were two opposing architectural viewpoints. The engineer-architect was mainly concerned with how to build with the new materials available, while the traditional architect continued to copy the forms of the past. But a brand new element settled the argument and made it obvious that the new age would have a style uniquely its own. This element was reinforced concrete.

By 1880, fairly large structures were being built with a steel framework. But steel wasn't fireproof and would warp under very intense heat. Reinforced concrete, "reinforced" because it had steel in it, solved this problem.

Building with reinforced concrete had obvious advantages. It was not only fire-resistant, it was resistant to the stresses of compression and tension and was inexpensive as well. Later it became possible to fold the steel rods inside the concrete, which increased its strength.

Stylistically, reinforced concrete had another advantage. It assumed the form of the mold from which it was taken. This malleability gave the architect the ability to create new forms. This was important in the development of arched bridges, such as Maillart's famous bridge of Salzinatobel.

Two Great Men: Wright and Le Corbusier

Many twentieth-century architects are worthy to stand alongside the great names of the past. But the two with the greatest influence on the twentieth century were the American Frank Lloyd Wright and the Swiss Le Corbusier, men who had almost opposing architectural philosophies.

Wright was born in Wisconsin in 1869 and grew up with a love for the country and a respect for nature, which had an impact on his work. Wright learned his craft in Chicago under an urban architect, Louis Sullivan, but he soon developed his own style. Rather than building great urban structures, he dedicated himself to designing private homes.

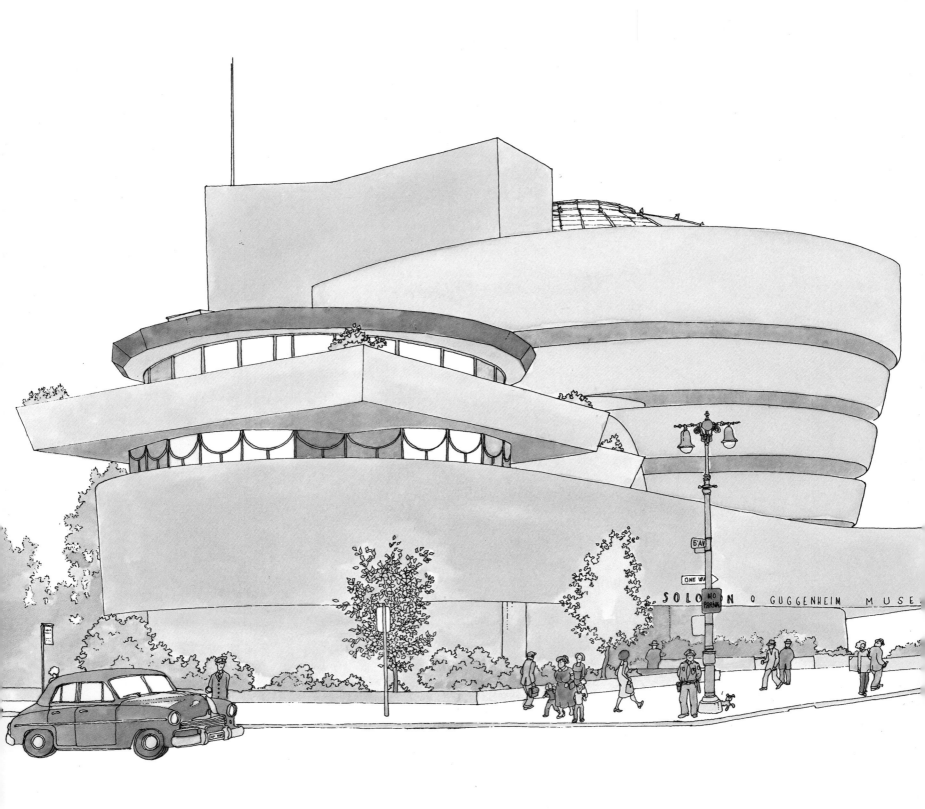

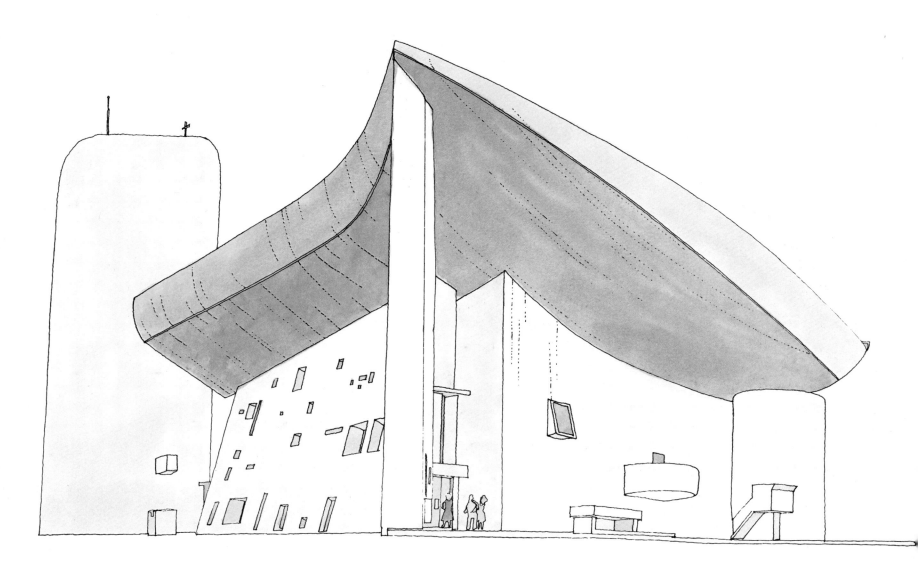

In these "prairie houses," he sought to do away with the distinction between inside and outside by means of terraces and horizontal roofs and by building with brick and wood. A famous example of the way he integrated nature in his designs is the house called "Falling Water," in Bear Run, Pa., which is literally built on a waterfall.

As time went on, Wright began to design public buildings as well, such as the Guggenheim Museum in New York. Construction on the Guggenheim Museum was begun in 1957 and finished in 1959, the year Wright died.

Le Corbusier's work is in direct contrast to the work of Wright. Le Corbusier, who was born at La Chaux-de-Fonds in 1887, was considered the greatest champion of geometrical and rational ideals. He expressed these ideals in his books and in his works, and above all, in a project which was called "La Ville Radieuse," which means "the radiant city."

Le Corbusier, who built the unique chapel shown here, Notre-Dame du Hant, in 1950, was the twentieth-century prophet of what lay ahead for the future—enormous, densely populated high-rise apartments.

New York, New York

As the population of a city increases, space becomes more and more precious. At the end of the nineteenth century, architects were already realizing that buildings had to occupy the least amount of space and yet house the maximum number of people. They would have to build up. It was the invention of the steam-powered elevator in 1861 that allowed men to build the first fifteen-floor high-rise building in Chicago. It was

also in Chicago that the architect Louis Sullivan built the first skyscrapers at the end of the nineteenth century.

With the coming of steel as an architectural material, skyscrapers really took off, and with glass they became transparent. Now buildings were so high they could cause vertigo. In the twentieth century, New York became a city of skyscrapers. In the 1920s, Wall Street was a jungle of soaring edifices. When the Empire State Building, which was 1,250 feet (370 meters) high, was finished in 1931, it was the tallest building in the world. Today, when we think of a city that symbolizes the modern world, we think of New York and its towering skyscrapers.

Brasilia

The fascination for building new cities has been experienced throughout history. For the United States it was Washington, D.C.; for Russia it was St. Petersburg; for Australia it was Canberra; for India it was New Delhi.

The new city which has most recently caught our attention is Brasilia, the capital of Brazil, one of the world's largest countries. Although the idea for Brasilia goes back to the beginning of the nineteenth century, it wasn't until the end of that century that people began to look for a suitable site. In the late 1950s, Brasilia was finally begun on a plateau at an elevation of 3,900 feet (1200 meters) in the Brazilian interior.

The plan, which was drawn up by Lúcio Costa, was striking. The principal buildings were planned by Oscar Niemeyer and were so unusual that they, too, created a sensation. The high, twin towers of the Congress, and the strange "upturned plate" of the House of Deputies, were built in Three Powers Plaza.

Brasilia, which was inaugurated in 1960, has a network of urban roads, but it still has far fewer inhabitants than the 800,000 foreseen by its planners. There are some who consider Brasilia to be a model for the future, while others criticize it as a symptom of the government's preoccupation with grandeur.

Sport Demands Space

During the last few decades, architects have wrestled with a problem the Romans wrestled with 2,000 years ago—the need to create huge structures for sports which can accommodate tens of thousands of spectators.

Modern architects have learned from the lessons of ancient Rome. After all, the Circus Maximus, where horse races were held, was nearly 2,000 feet (600 meters) long, 660 feet (200 meters) wide, and could hold 350,000 spectators.

When the Olympics resumed after World War II, contemporary architects were in the position of having to build huge sports complexes. These were true "sport cities" made up of various buildings and stadiums that required sophisticated and advanced designs. The great Japanese architect Kenzo Tange designed the stadium, which is shown here, for the 1964 Tokyo Olympics. Because Japan is one of the world's foremost industrial nations, Tange tried in his work to reconcile Japanese tradition with the urban needs of an advanced country.

Buildings for New Worlds

When the explorer James Cook landed in Australia in April 1770, he was one of the first Europeans ever to set foot on that land. And to Cook's company, it seemed like a very strange land indeed, with some of the most primitive people in the world and animals such as the kangaroo, which was able to leap more than 20 feet (7 meters) on strong back legs.

Now, two hundred years later, the traveler no longer finds a deserted coast populated only by marsupials. Today he finds thriving cities with millions of inhabitants. Melbourne hosted the Olympic games, and Sydney's Opera House, shown here, is one of the most fascinating complexes in modern architecture. Designed by Jørn Utzon and begun in 1959, its ''sails'' seem to soar out over the bay.

Like Australia, there are other countries where western culture has been flourishing only a short time but which have already achieved a significant architectural sophistication. Certainly the trapper who crossed the snowy wastes of Canada in the last century could never have imagined the complexity of a city like modern Montreal.

The Triumph of the Skyscraper

Every era has been characterized by a particular architectural style. We speak of the Gothic age, the Palladian age, the Baroque age, and so on. This is possible because we are distant in time from those periods. Certainly no builder would have said to himself, "I live in the Gothic age." Only as time passes do we characterize an architectural period and give it a name.

So what can we call our own architectural period? The twentieth century has seen many important movements, such as Bauhaus, Rationalism, Constructivism. Despite all this variety, we do have one

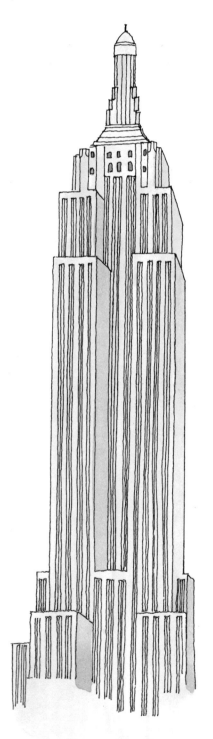

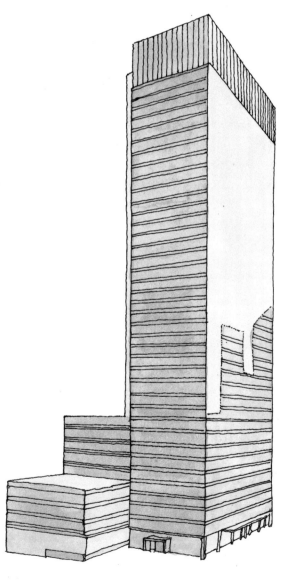

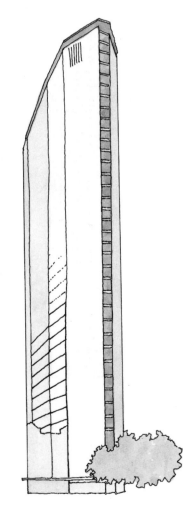

The Empire State Building

The Seagram Building

The Pirelli skyscraper

common and very visible symbol that unites our era. That is the skyscraper, which is to be found all over the world.

We are constantly building higher and higher. The twin towers of the World Trade Center in New York are 1,300 feet (400 meters) high. Mies van der Rohe's Seagram Building in New York is not only high but beautiful as well. The Pirelli building in Milan, a work of Pier Luigi Nervi and Gio Ponti, is also a fine example of a modern skyscraper.

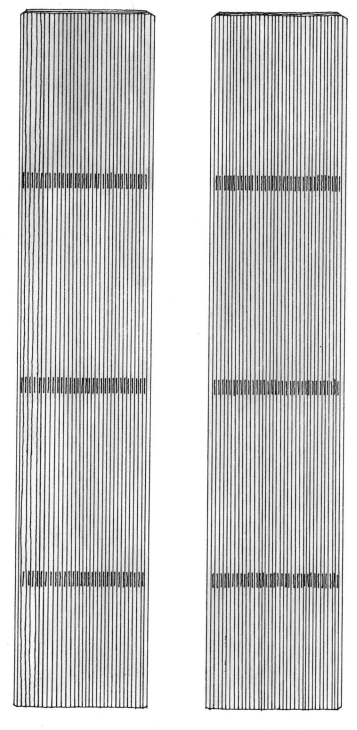

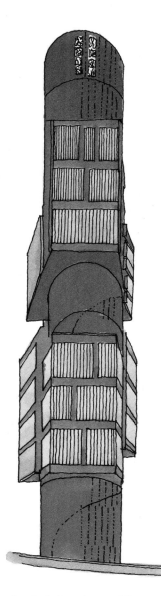

The twin towers of the World Trade Center

The administrative offices of Shizuoka

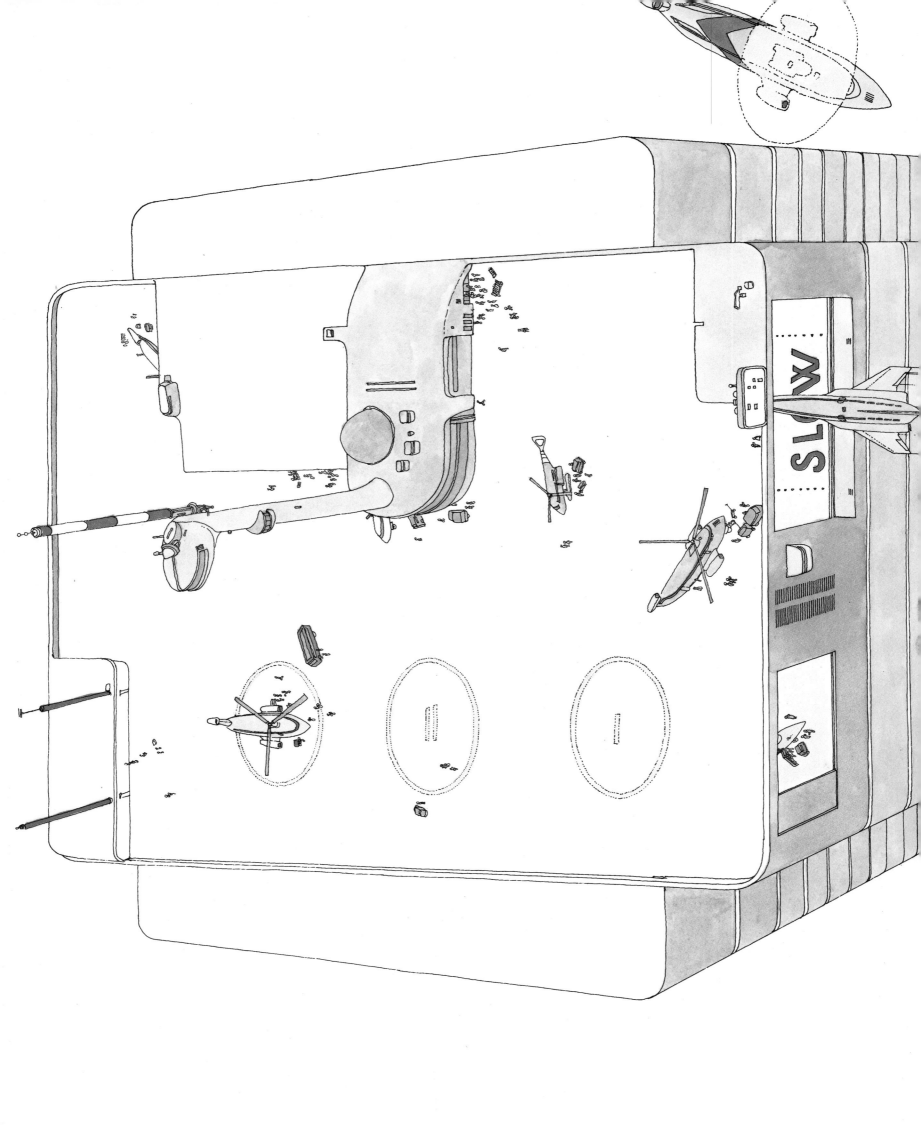

Where To Go?

If it is difficult to define our own era, it is even more difficult to foresee the future. However, we can make some educated guesses. In the year 2000, there will be about 7 billion people on earth. Because space will become more and more precious, we will have to build higher and higher.

Unlike our buildings of the past, our future skyscrapers will be built for reasons of economy, not grandeur. But where will we end up? Years ago, Frank Lloyd Wright planned the 3,000-foot skyscraper, a real monster! Here an even taller building is pictured, suitable for a time when more and more people will have to live in high-rise structures.

Language of Architecture

Amphitheater. A theater with an oval plan consisting of an interior of rows of steps rising from ground level and an exterior of three stories of arcades. Typically Roman, the design spread throughout the empire during the early centuries A.D. An example is the Colosseum in Rome.

Apse. The semicircular or many-sided projection at the termination of the longitudinal axis of a basilica, covered by a half dome or a vault.

Arch. A curved structure composed of blocks of building material, usually wedge-shaped, spanning an opening. The curve of the arch transfers the thrust and weight downward and outward onto the supporting columns or piers. May also be called a curved lintel, although it is not composed of a monolithic block as is a lintel.
Round arch: a semicircular arch, preferred by the Romans.
Pointed arch: formed by two curves that meet at the apex. Taller than a round arch, the pointed arch was used in Gothic architecture to achieve extremely high vaults.

Architrave. Two upright posts or columns support a third post or column which is laid horizontally across them. This third post is called the lintel, or architrave, and the whole construction is called the post and lintel system. If composed of an inflexible material such as stone, the architrave must be short, but if composed of a material such as steel, the architrave can span far greater openings.

Baptistery. The building which contains the baptismal font. Originally, the baptistery was situated in front of or alongside the cathedral to emphasize the need for baptism in order to be admitted into the Church. Normally circular or many-sided, the baptistery is covered by a dome or a pitched roof.

Bay. Any large division in a structure or building, such as the space created between columns or pillars.

Buttress. A thick structure built against a wall to give it added stability. In Gothic architecture, a series of buttresses on the exterior walls helped support the weight of the vaults.
Flying buttress: An exposed arch on the upper exterior of a Gothic cathedral which carries the weight and thrust of the vault over the roof of the side aisles down onto the buttresses of the outside walls.

Capital. The head or uppermost part of a column or pillar, on which the lintel rests. According to its style it can assume different shapes.

Caryatid. A draped female form with a cushion on her head, sometimes used in Greece instead of a column to support the entablature.

Castrum. The plan of Roman towns and military camps. The streets form a right-angle grid pattern with a square, or forum, in the center. Later, the term came to mean a fortified town or castle.

Centering. Wood or iron scaffolding used to set bricks or stones when building an arch or a vault. The centering is removed once the mortar has set.

Choir. Space in front of the church altar reserved for the singers. Normally it is raised by steps above the floor of the nave, or by a whole flight of steps when it overhangs a crypt. The term also refers to the complex of wooden seats for the singers, or monks, which is sometimes located in the apse.

Cloister. Open space surrounded by roofed porticoes, based on a quadrangle plan. The cloister was attached to a church with an annexed abbey or convent. Because cloisters typically are within monasteries, the word has come to mean the monastery itself.

Column. An upright shaft or pillar, usually circular and made of stone. It is topped by a capital and rests on the floor (Doric column) or on a base. If the column is fluted, it appears slim. If it tapers toward the top, it appears taller. A sequence of columns surmounted by an entablature or arcade forms an order. According to the style of the column and its capital, orders are termed Doric, Ionic, Corinthian or "composite." Doric columns are squat and massive. The others rest on thin bases and are slender. Throughout the history of architecture, interlaced and spiral columns were also used, the latter typical of the Baroque style.

Corbel. A piece of stone, wood or iron projecting from the vertical part of a structure, wall or pillar. The corbel supports an object which rests upon it. Often a decoration conceals its support function.

Crossing. The point within a church at which nave and transept intersect. The crossing point is often covered by a dome. Churches formed by two intersecting rectangles are called cross-shaped. When the arms of the cross are the same size, we say a church has a Greek cross plan. When the nave is longer than the transept, it is called a Latin cross plan.

Crypt. The word derives from the Greek and means "hidden, subterranean place." The crypt is that part of Early Christian, Romanesque and Gothic basilicas beneath the choir, or presbytery, where the relics of Christian martyrs were preserved.

Dome. A large hemispherical or approximately hemispherical roof over buildings which have central or cross-shaped plans. Domes, which are common in Byzantine architecture, were the basis for the Islamic mosque. The Romans used the dome first, that of the Pantheon being the most famous in antiquity.

Drum. The circular or many-sided wall that links the dome to the supporting piers and arches.

Entablature. The whole of the superstructure supported by the columns in the classical temple. The entablature consists of architrave (the original beam running from support to support), frieze (the central beam, above the architrave), pediment (the triangular section below the roof and above the frieze), and cornice (the topmost part, formed of a series of moldings that project from the face of the frieze).

Jamb. A side or vertical piece of any opening in a wall, door, window, or fireplace.

Keystone. The stone at the apex of an arch. The keystone, which is the last stone laid, locks the whole arch in place.

Lantern. A small tower with windows that often tops the dome. The lantern admits light high over the crossing and altar.

Lintel. Horizontal post laid across two upright posts, forming the post and lintel system.

Lunette. A surface of semicircular shape in a vaulted ceiling, wall, or on a portal. It is often decorated by a painting or bas-relief.

Mold. The form constructed by wood, iron, or plastic into which concrete is poured. Concrete, made by mixing cement, sand, and rubble with water (and in modern times often reinforced with iron or steel rods), can assume an infinite variety of shapes according to the shape of the mold. When the concrete has hardened, the mold is removed.

Mullioned window. Multiple-arched window on Romanesque and Gothic buildings. In later periods, mullioned windows became large and elaborate, with tracery work and stained glass.

Nave. The central longitudinal aisle of the Early Christian basilica or of any church unless it is built on a centralized plan. Often the nave is flanked on each side by one or two aisles.

Obelisk. Typical monument of Egypt, formed by a slim, tall monolith with the cusp originally gold-plated. Only four still remain in Egypt.

Pediment. The triangular section below the roof and above the frieze on the façade of a classical temple. The pediment is usually adorned with sculptural decoration.

Pillar or pier. An upright support with quadrangular, polygonal, or circular section, resting on a base called the plinth. In Gothic architecture, the pillar became very elaborate, sometimes assuming the form of a bundle of columns.

Rib. The supporting and decorative part of a vault or dome. The rib carries the weight down to the pier shaft or walls. It can assume elaborate forms.

Rose window. A large circular window on the upper façade of Romanesque and Gothic churches, divided by mullions or tracery radiating from the center and often finely decorated with stained glass.

Rustication. The masonry construction of a wall in which the individual blocks are heavily emphasized and project out in relief from the wall surface. Rustication was frequently used on the ground floor of Renaissance and Baroque palaces for a grandiose effect.

Transept. The arm of a cruciform church perpendicular to the central nave. It usually separates the nave from the choir and apse. Some churches have multiple transepts and the transept itself can have aisles.

Truss. A combination of beams, bars, or ties arranged in a triangle to form a rigid framework as a support for the roof.

Vault. An arched ceiling. The fundamental type of vault results from the longitudinal progression of an arch (barrel vault). Two intersecting barrel vaults form a cross, or groin, vault. When the vault is the result of an ogive arch, it is called an ogival vault.

Architects

Aalto, Alvar (1898–1976) stands out among rationalist architects for the malleable note he introduced in his works—curved walls, overhanging stairs, corrugated façades, all of which were conceived with a pure line. He also popularized wood by using it in totally new ways and forms. He worked in America, the Far East, and Europe. In Italy, his last work was the church of Riola near Bologna. He was also concerned with town planning, as can be seen in his plans for Helsinki.

Alberti, Leon Battista (1404–1472) embodied the ideal of the cultured and refined Renaissance man. He broke with Gothic tradition, returning instead to the classical Greek and Roman world. A great architectural theoretician, he wrote the treatise *De re aedificatoria*. Although few of the works he designed were actually built, they were all masterpieces—for example, the Tempio Malatestiano at Rimini and the church of Sant'Andrea at Mantua.

Bernini, Giovanni Lorenzo (1598–1680) was the ultimate representative of the Roman Baroque style. During his long career, he served seven popes. His first work at St. Peter's was the baldachin for the high altar, in which he blended sculpture and architecture. The vast colonnade of St. Peter's Square best demonstrates Bernini's magnificent and exuberant style.

Borromini, Francesco (1599–1667), who was the genius of the Baroque, is usually mentioned with Bernini. But the two, after a long collaboration, became fierce rivals. A restless and lonely character, Borromini created works of exceptional originality and beauty, such as the churches of San Carlo alle Quattro Fontane and Sant'Ivo alla Sapienza in which fantasy combines with rigid geometrical plans to create spatial compositions of great liveliness.

Bramante, Donato (1444–1514), who assimilated the lessons of early Renaissance architects, developed his own enduring and magnificent style. He worked mainly in Rome under Pope Julius II, who commissioned, among other works, the rebuilding of St. Peter's basilica.

Brunelleschi, Filippo (1377–1446) created a new style, free of Gothic forms. Although his Ospedale degli Innocenti is the first recorded Renaissance building, Brunelleschi's name is associated principally with the dome of Santa Maria del Fiore, the cathedral of Florence. The churches of San Lorenzo and Santo Spirito, the Pazzi Chapel, and the Pitti Palace, all also in Florence, are his finest works.

Buonarroti, Michelangelo (1475–1564) united painting, sculpture and architecture in a superb harmony. Among his buildings are the Biblioteca Laurenziana and the Medici Chapel in Florence. By modifying already classical Renaissance forms, he gave dramatic and renewed life to every project he undertook.

Cortona, Pietro da (1596–1669) entered the circle of Cardinal Barberini as soon as he arrived in Rome. As a result, he was awarded important commissions. Among his most important works was the church of SS. Luca e Martina, which is considered to be the first great Baroque church. From a rather free and animated style, he eventually moved toward more rigid and somber forms.

Gaudi, Antoni (1852–1926), in the beginning of this century, was at the forefront of the revolution in architecture, as Picasso was at the forefront of the revolution in painting. Gaudí elaborated and modified Gothic and Moorish styles into fantastic inventions. His most famous work, the church of the Sagrada Familia in Barcelona, is one of the most baffling buildings in the world.

Gropius, Walter (1883–1969) is the supreme representative of European rationalism. His name was tied to the Bauhaus of Weimar which he founded, built and directed until 1928. Here architecture was considered the synthesis of all the arts, with the artist pledging to devote himself to every object produced by industry. Thus, "industrial design" was born. During the Nazi period, Gropius became a professor at Harvard University.

Jones, Inigo (1573–1652), already distinguished at the English court as a scenographer, was appointed Superintendent of the King's Buildings in 1615. He revolutionized English architecture by introducing Italian classicism, particularly the Palladian style which he interpreted and adapted to English needs. Thus, it was he who inspired the Palladianism which reigned in both England and America in the 18th century.

Le Corbusier (1887–1965) was the pseudonym for the Swiss architect Charles-Édouard Jeanneret. Le Corbusier elaborated and spread the ideas of rationalism abroad, that is, an architecture completely free from traditional styles and considered to be a perfect machine for human habitation. Town planning along rational and functional lines also owes much to Le Corbusier. His vision, however, did not prevent him from designing poetic and important works independent from rational formalism. His most famous works remain the Unité d'Habitation, a large apartment complex at Marseilles; the chapel at Ronchamp; the convent of La Tourette near Lyon; the plan of Chandigarh in India; and the United Nations building in New York, which was a committee project.

Maderno, Carlo (1556–1629), who was born at Lake Lugano, settled in 1588 in Rome, where he was given the difficult task of lengthening the basilica of St. Peter's. Bramante had originally designed the basilica with a centralized plan which was subsequently altered by Michelangelo. We also owe the façade to Maderno.

Maillart, Robert (1872–1940), Swiss architect and engineer, developed all the technical and aesthetic possibilities of concrete, devoting himself above all to building bridges.

Mies van der Rohe, Ludwig (1886–1969), who was in agreement with Gropius's rationalistic concepts, succeeded Gropius as director of the Bauhaus. With the German Pavilion for the Barcelona Exhibition in 1929, Mies van der Rohe revealed his search for pure composition and the perfect use of materials. He continued to pursue this search in America, where he had migrated during the Nazi regime, with his plan for the campus of the Illinois Institute of Technology. In Chicago and New York, he carried this out further, with steel and glass towers of exceptional grace.

Nervi, Pier Luigi (1891–1979) was educated as an engineer and, in fact, an engineer's structural viewpoint prevails in his works. He was able to model concrete as few others could, with original technical and expressive creations. He built many sports complexes, exhibition centers, and wide halls like the audience hall in the Vatican, as well as the structural frame of the Pirelli skyscraper in Milan. He often worked in both America and France.

Neumann, Johann Balthasar (1687–1753) was the highest exponent of German Rococo. He devoted himself primarily to building princely palaces with monumental and elaborate staircases. In sacred architecture, he gave free play to his lively imagination, attaining a complex, refined and sometimes frivolous style.

Niemeyer, Oscar (1907–   ) lives in Rio de Janeiro in one of his own fascinating buildings. In 1957, he was called upon to direct the planning of Brasilia, where he designed the hotel, the presidential palace and, as his supreme work, the Three Powers Plaza. In the Three Powers Plaza, a dome and a bowl (Senate and Chamber) emerge from a plate entered by an enormous ramp. At the center, two parallel towers of government offices rise up.

Palladio, Andrea (1508–1580) was one of the greatest of all Italian architects, with a lasting influence in Europe and America. He became famous not only by winning the competition for the Basilica of Vicenza, but also for his city palaces and country villas on the Venetian mainland. He built churches in Venice as well, and with the publication of the *Four Books on Architecture* proved himself to be a major theoretician.

Peruzzi, Baldassare (1481–1536), who was originally a painter in Siena, worked mainly in Rome where he participated in the building of St. Peter's. He owed much to Raphael and Bramante, although his style was more refined and less solemn. His first major work was the Farnesina, and his last the Palazzo Massimo alle Colonne, in which he expressed a mannered style.

Ponti, Gio (1891–1979) left his mark in a whole variety of objects in the field of industrial design. As an architect in Italy, he was one of the pioneers of rationalism. His most interesting building is the Pirelli skyscraper in Milan, which owes its structural frame to Nervi.

Saarinen, Eero (1910–1961), an internationally educated Finn, followed rationalism at first, then began to experiment with original structures and design. His air terminal buildings are particularly interesting: the TWA Terminal at Kennedy Airport in New York and Dulles Airport in Washington, D.C.

Sangallo, Antonio da (1483–1546), called Sangallo the Younger, is from a family of architects, and one of the major representatives of the Renaissance in Rome. He worked on St. Peter's basilica, modifying the preceding project. Also by Sangallo is Palazzo Farnese, later completed by Michelangelo.

Scamozzi, Vincenzo (1552–1616) was the best known of Palladio's followers. Although he worked almost exclusively in Venice and in the Veneto, he also traveled throughout Europe, leaving behind several projects. He wrote the treatise *The Idea of Universal Architecture.*

Sullivan, Louis Henri (1856–1924) was one of the greatest representatives of the so-called Chicago School which marks the birth of modern architecture in America and its separation from European tradition. His most famous skyscrapers, the Wainwright Building in St. Louis (1890) and the Guaranty Building in Buffalo (1894), although elaborate in decoration, succeeded in clearly expressing the main structural lines and the functional distribution of spaces.

Tange, Kenzo (1913–) is now considered one of the greatest living architects, not only in Japan, but also in the West. Together with Japanese engineers, he combines structural research with the study of highly expressive and sometimes amazing forms and compositions. He conducts programs on town planning at Tokyo University, and in 1960 he proposed a mega-structure for the capital which, resting on pillars that emerged from the sea, extended into the bay.

Utzon, Jørn (1918–), a Danish architect, is universally known for the Sydney Opera House, an exceptional building that resembles a ship leaving the harbor under full sail. For the design of the building's bold vaults, he worked with another Danish architect, Ove Nyquist Arup, who devised this original use for reinforced concrete.

Vinci, Leonardo da (1452–1519) was *the* genius of Renaissance art and science. As an architect, he greatly influenced Bramante. Although he drew up many plans, such as those for an ideal town and the dome of Milan Cathedral, none of them was carried out. His study of statics—the physical laws that govern bodies at rest or in equilibrium—was especially important, and he can be considered a pioneer in the study of building materials.

Wren, Christopher (1632–1723), the greatest English architect, was a professor of astronomy until the 1666 London fire. Although his plans for rebuilding London were rejected as being too utopian, he devoted himself to rebuilding approximately fifty churches. To this day, his masterpiece remains St. Paul's Cathedral. He relied on classical style but enriched it with both Baroque elements and his own original modifications.

Wright, Frank Lloyd (1869–1959) is generally recognized as the greatest American architect and one of the supreme masters of all time. He began as a pupil of Sullivan, designing single residences in the Chicago area and in California which settled naturally into their settings. "Falling Water," his house at Bear Run, Pennsylvania, is the nearest he ever came to embracing European rationalism. His most important works date from the last twenty years of his life: the Guggenheim Museum in New York, the Unitarian Church in Madison, Wisconsin, and the office-skyscraper in Bartlesville, Oklahoma.

Illustrations